Editorial Project Manager
Mara Ellen Guckian

Editor-in-Chief
Sharon Coan, M.S. Ed.

Illustrator
Alexandra Artigas

Cover Artist
Brenda DiAntonis

Art Coordinator
Kevin Barnes

Art Director
Cjae Froshay

Imaging
Ralph Olmedo, Jr.

Product Manager
Phil Garcia

Publisher
Mary D. Smith, M.S. Ed.

Numbers, Shapes, & Colors

Red

Yellow

Diamond

Circle

Four Fish

Five Green Gumballs

Author

Krista Pettit

Teacher Created Resources

Teacher Created Resources, Inc.
6421 Industry Way
Westminster, CA 92683
www.teachercreated.com
ISBN-0-7439-3230-7
©2003 Teacher Created Resources, Inc.
Reprinted, 2005
Made in U.S.A.

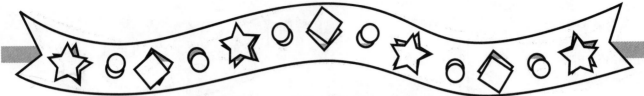

Table of Contents

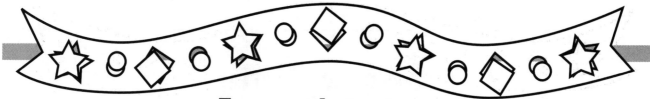

Introduction

Getting children ready for academic success starts early. It is important, in these early years, to shape children's attitudes towards school and learning in a positive way. The ultimate purpose of this series of work books is to promote children's development and learning in an exciting manner. Young children need lots of repetition and simply worded directions. The activities need to be enjoyable and visually stimulating. This series was developed with those goals in mind. Each activity book is designed to introduce young learners to new concepts and to reinforce ones already learned. The pages are great for enrichment, classroom practice, tutoring, home schooling, or just for fun.

In *Numbers, Shapes, & Colors* students will focus on the following concepts:

- **Numbers:** While completing the number activities, children will review number recognition, counting, and the concepts of "more than" and "less than."

- **Shapes:** The shape activities help to reinforce the identification of triangles, squares, rectangles, and circles.

- **Colors:** Children will learn to identify color names, to color using color keys, and to sort by color.

Parents can also use this workbook series to reinforce skills learned at home and/or school. Completing these workbook pages together with their parents allows youngsters the opportunity to practice newly acquired knowledge in a stress-free environment. Some of the activities require cutting and pasting. Copying the cutting and pasting pages onto card stock or heavy paper will assist beginning cutters by providing a sturdier material to grasp and manipulate.

The workbooks in this series will enhance children's abilities to retain newly obtained concepts and skills by providing them with exciting workbook pages on which they can practice. Utilizing these workbook pages for seat work, homework, or home practice makes these books a versatile resource which can benefit children in a variety of environments. With a user-friendly layout, these workbook pages allow children to follow the easy-to-read directions, and to enjoy the practice. This type of independent work allows children to internalize new concepts in a fun and meaningful way.

Name_____

Snack Time

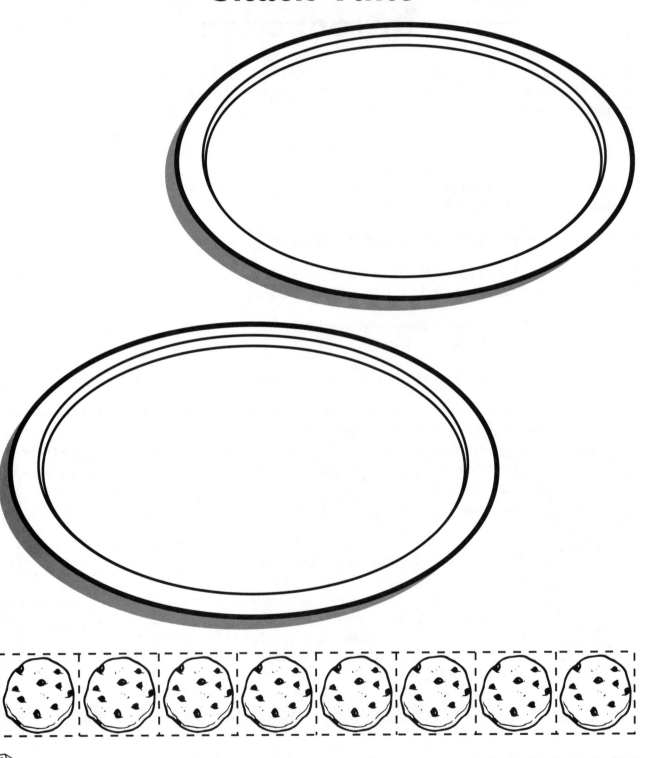

Directions: Help share the cookies. Cut out each cookie and glue it onto a plate until each plate has an equal number of cookies.

Name_____

Block Time

Directions: Color and cut out the blocks. Glue the blocks in the box above in an interesting way.

Name_____

What's Missing?

 1    2    3

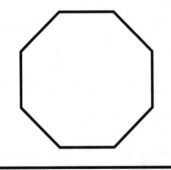 5       7    8

    3    4    5

 7   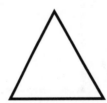 8       10

 3   ▲   5   6

• •

Directions: Fill in the missing numbers in each row.

Buggy Numbers

	8		4
	7		1
	2		5
	6		3

Directions: Look at the number in each box. Finish each bug by drawing that number of wings on the bug. The first one is done for you. Color the bugs.

Out of Order

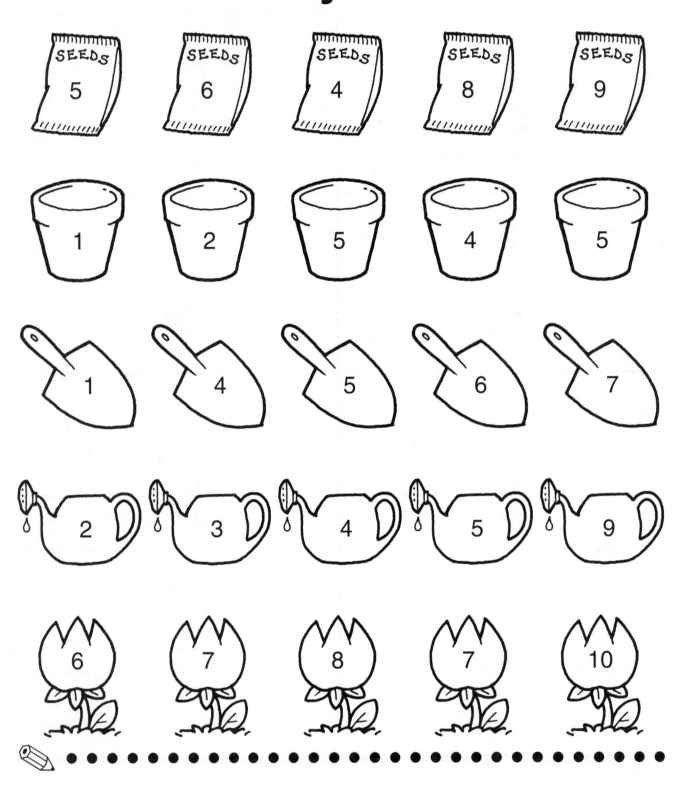

Directions: Cross out the number that does not belong in each row of garden items. Write the correct number above the item.

Name_____

Fishy Counting

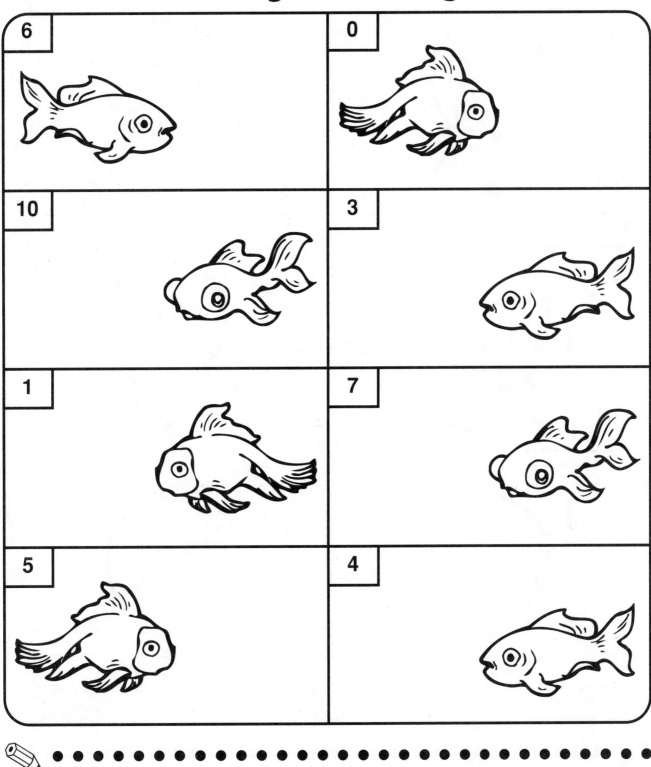

Directions: Look at the number in the box at the top left of each square. Draw that many bubbles for the fish.

Name_____

Guess and Count

Guess   Count

Guess   Count

Guess   Count

Guess   Count

Guess   Count

Guess   Count

Directions: Guess how many gumballs are in each jar and write the number on the line.
Then count the gumballs and write the actual number on the second line in the box.

Name_____

Lunch Time

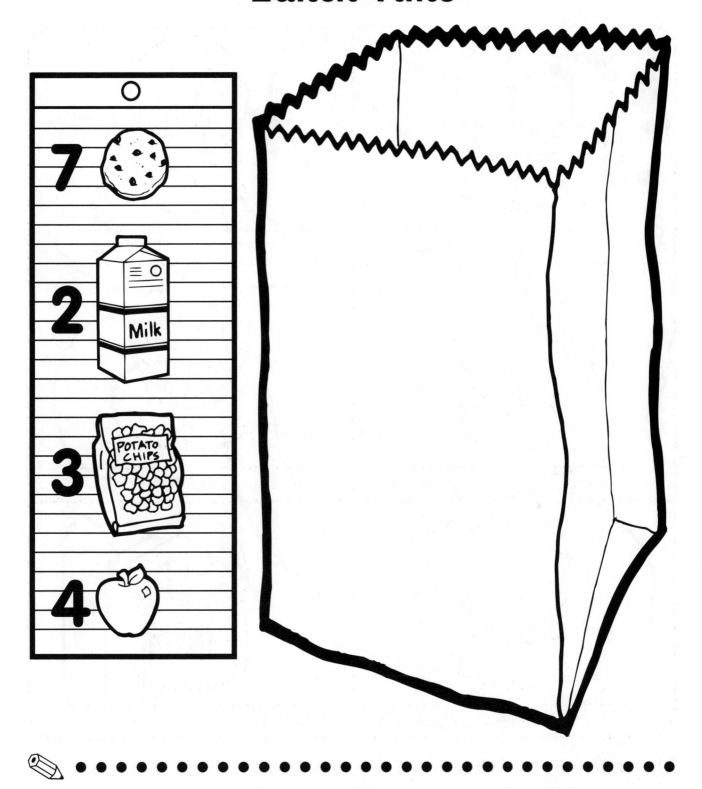

Directions: After reading the lunch order on the left, draw the number of objects onto the lunch bag.

Name_____

Help the Cow

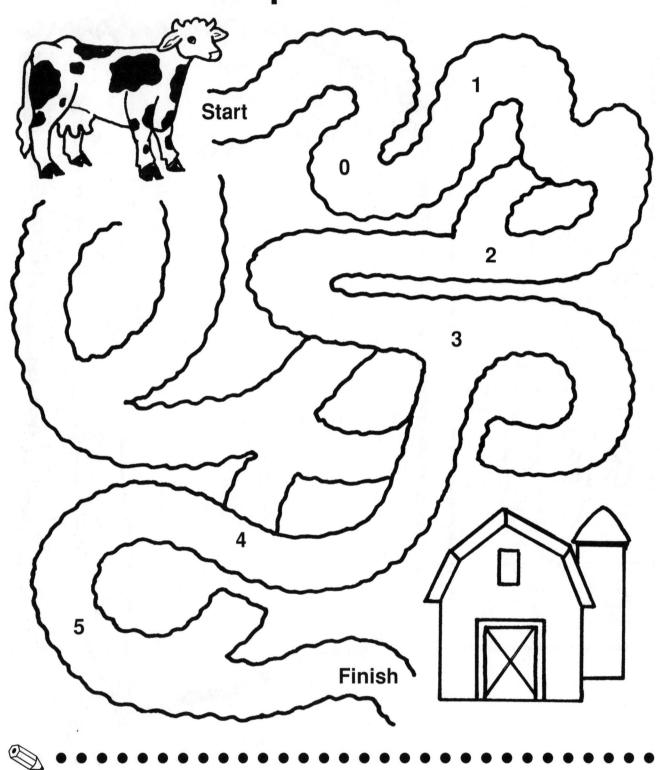

Start

0

1

2

3

4

5

Finish

#3230 Numbers, Shapes, & Colors

Directions: Complete the maze and help the cow get back to the barn. Follow the numbers in order through the maze.

Name_____

Find the Baby

Directions: Complete the maze and help the mother dinosaur find her baby. Follow the numbers in order through the maze. Begin with the number 5.

Name_____

Number Match

Pizza, Pizza!

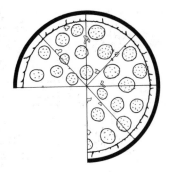

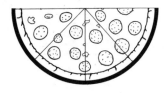

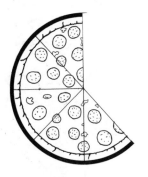
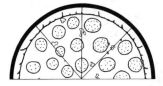

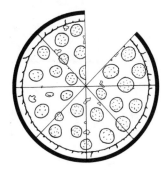

• •

Directions: Look at the pizzas in the column on the left. Find the missing slices in the column on the right. Draw a line from the pizzas on the left to the correct number of pizza slices on the right.

Name_____

Beach Finds

How many can you find?

 _____   _____   _____

 _____ ⛟ _____ ✦ _____

✏ •

Directions: Look at the list of items to find. Count the items and write the number on the line next to the picture. Color the picture.

On the Road

How many can you find?

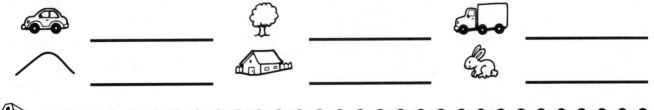

Directions: Look at the list of items to find. Count the items and write the number on the line next to the word. Color the picture.

Missing Pets

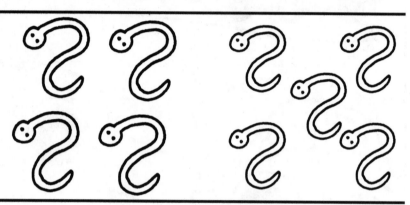

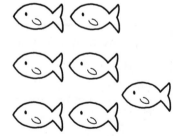

● ●

Directions: Look at each row. Draw the missing number of pets that fit in each sequence.

Name_____

Sailing Away

Directions: Cut out the boats. Glue the boats on top of the waters that contain the matching group of sea animals.

Name_____

Spotty Fun

Directions: Look at the number in each box. Add that number of spots to the animal. Color the animals.

Name_____

Animal Count

Directions: Look at the animals in each box. Write the number of animals in each space.

Name_____

Draw More

Draw one more.

Draw two more.

Directions: Look at the pictures on the left. Compare them to the pictures on the right. What is missing in the picture on the right? Follow the directions in each box to complete the pictures on the right.

Name_____

Draw Less

Draw one less.

Draw two less.

Directions: Look at the pictures on the left. Compare them to the pictures on the right. What is missing in the pictures on the right? Follow the directions in each box to complete the pictures on the right.

Name_____

Which Has More?

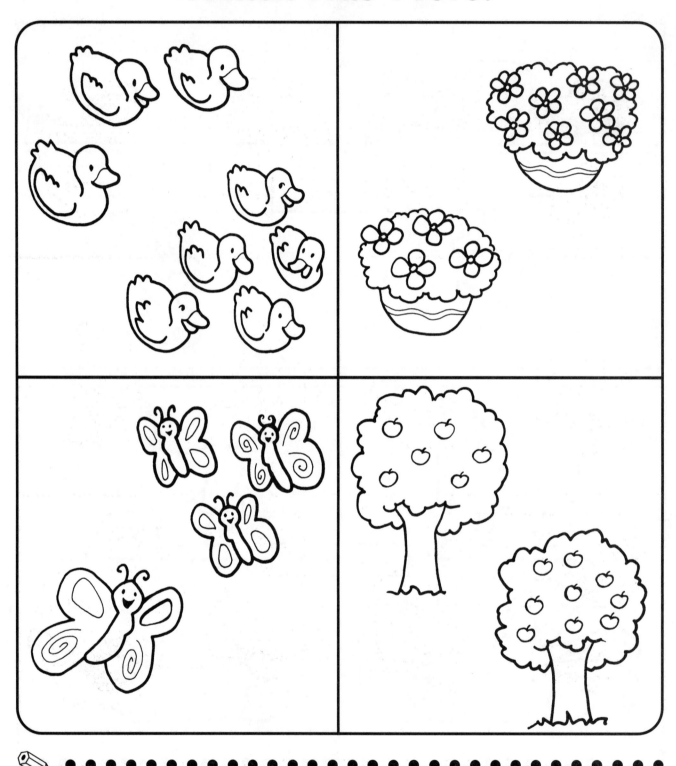

Directions: Circle the group in each box with a greater number of objects.

Which Has Less?

Directions: Circle the group in each box with the least number of objects or people.

Hungry Hippo

Directions: Draw a line from the hungry hippo to the greater amount of food. Color the hippo and the greater amount of food.

26

Phone Pad Math

 •

Directions: Circle all numbers greater than 6. Color all the numbers greater than 2.
Place an **X** on the numbers greater than 7.

Name_____

Call This Number

- Circle all numbers **less than** 5.
- Color all numbers **less than** 8.

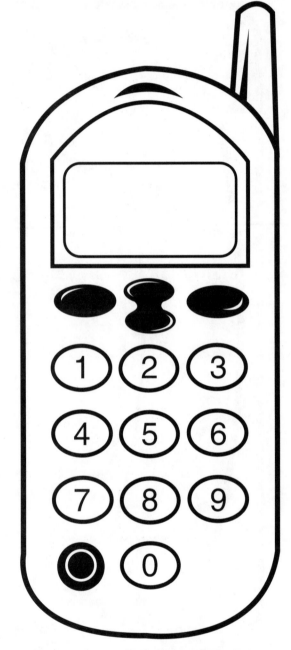

- Circle all numbers **less than** 7.
- Color all numbers **less than** 3.

 •

Directions: Follow the directions above for each phone.

Name_____

Butterfly Count

1 2 3   4 5 6

4 5 6   7 8 9

Directions: Add one more spot to each butterfly and circle the total number of spots.

Name_____

Calculate This

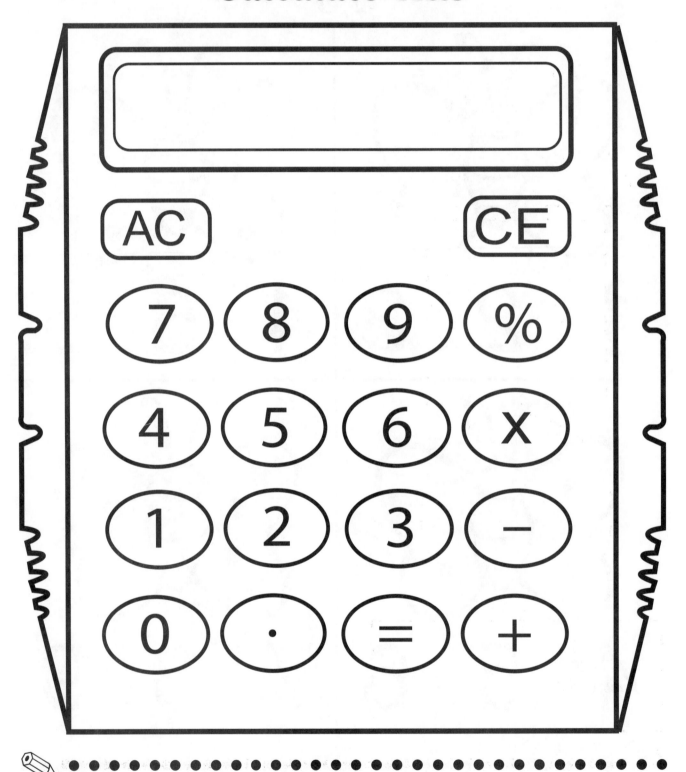

✏️ •••

Directions: Circle all numbers greater than 3. Cross out numbers less than 8.

Name_____

Shape Trace

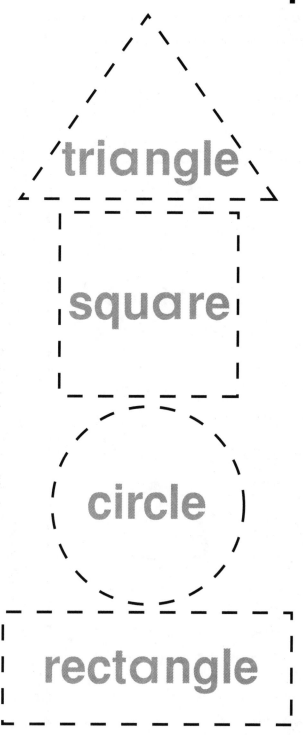

Directions: Trace each shape and the shape word. Draw each shape. Color each shape.

Name_____

More Shapes

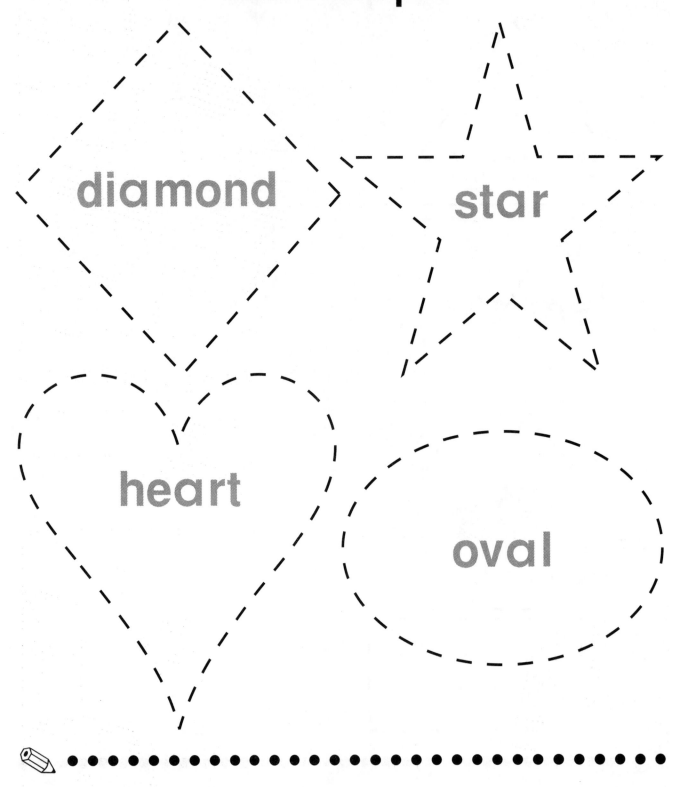

diamond

star

heart

oval

Directions: Trace each shape. Color each shape a different color.

Pretty Beads

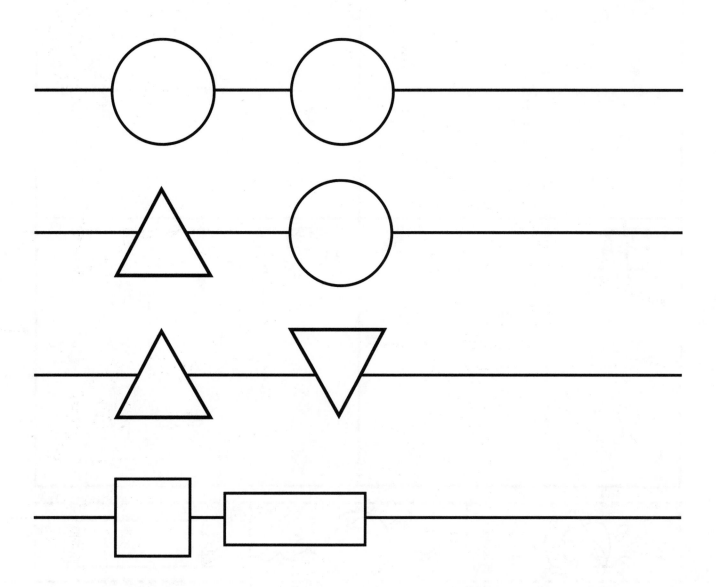

 •

Directions: Finish each necklace by adding the correct shapes to continue the pattern.
Color the necklaces.

Name_____

Beach Shapes

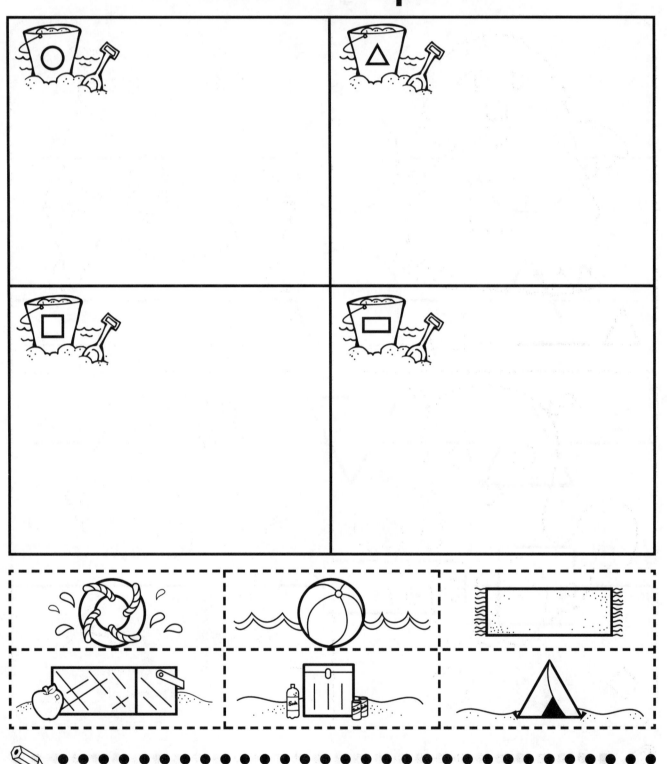

Directions: Look at the different shapes on each bucket. Cut out each beach object with the same shape and glue it below the correct bucket. Some boxes will have two pictures.

Name_____

Shapely Monsters

Directions: Count the number of shapes that makes up each monster. Write each answer on the line next to the shape.

Shape Riddles

1. I have no points.
   I have no straight lines.
   I am round.
   What am I?

2. I have straight sides.
   I have three points.
   What am I?

3. I have four sides.
   I have four points.
   I look like a box.
   What am I?

4. I have two points.
   I have rounded sides.
   When you see me,
   you think of love.
   What am I?

5. I have four sides.
   My sides are straight.
   I am not a square.
   What am I?

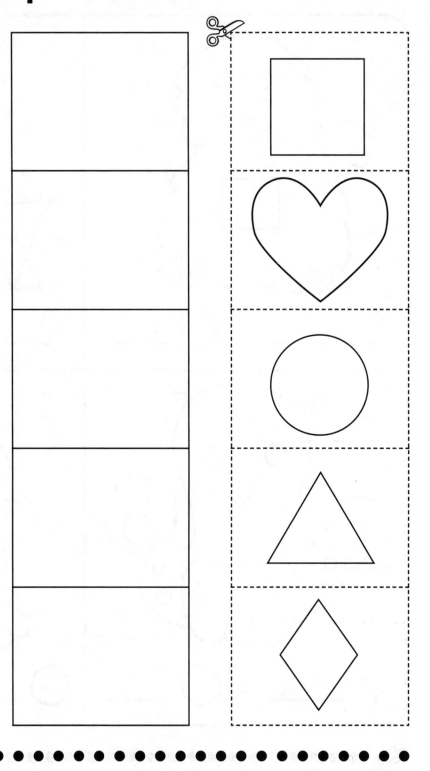

Directions: Color and cut out the shapes. Listen to the riddles. Paste each shape next to the riddle it matches.

Name_____

Create A Monster

Directions: Trace the shapes. Color the shapes. Cut out the shapes and glue them onto a piece of construction paper to create a funny monster. Add details.

Name_____

Merry Shapes

Directions: Cut out the shapes and glue them on or near the tree. Color the holiday scene.

Name_____

Color Words

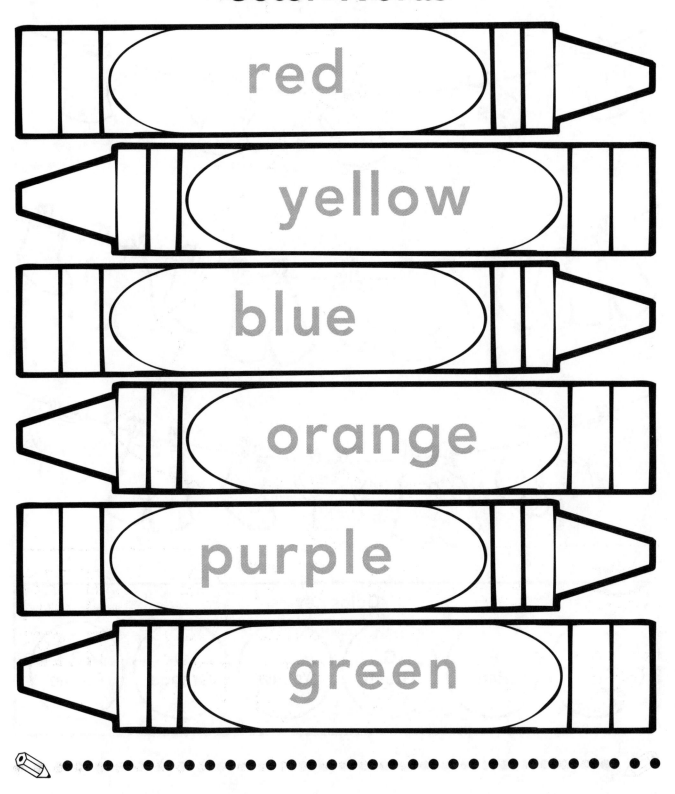

red

yellow

blue

orange

purple

green

Directions: Trace the color words in each crayon. Color the crayons to match the color words.

Name_____

Hangin' Patterns

Directions: Color the Color Key. Color the clothes on the lines using the Color Key. Continue each pattern for the rest of the clothes on the line.

Name_____

Color Continue

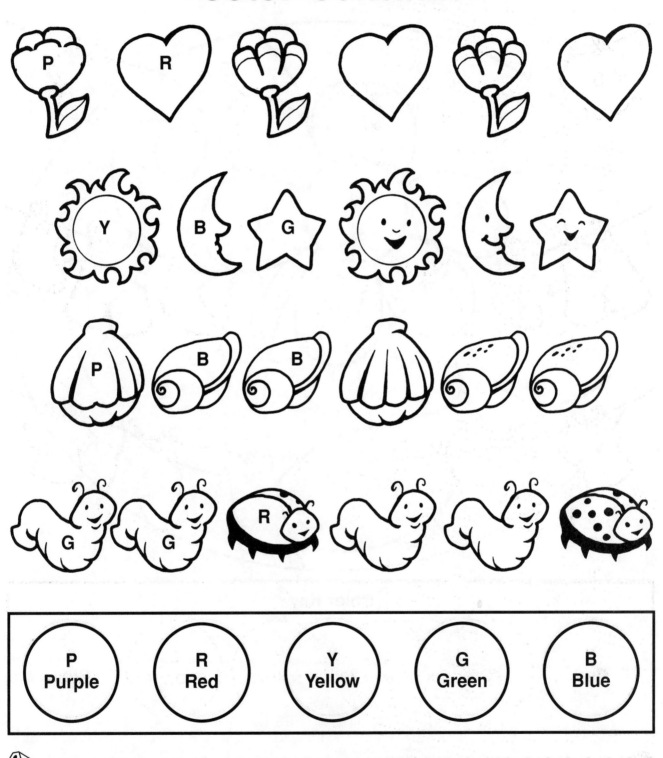

P	R	Y	G	B
Purple	Red	Yellow	Green	Blue

Directions: Color the Color Key. Follow the key to color each pattern and repeat it.

Name_____

Stained Glass Picture

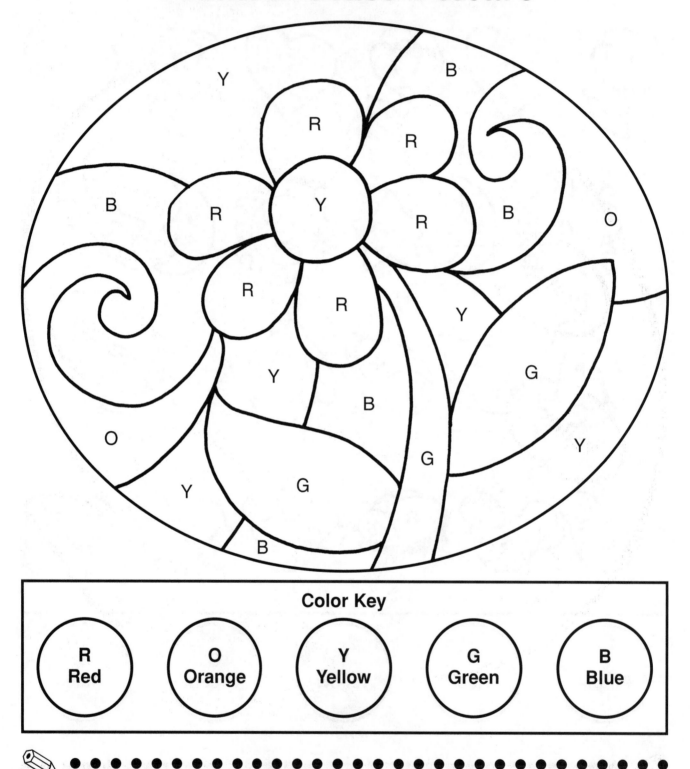

Directions: Color the Color Key. Color each section of stained glass picture using the Color Key. What do you see?

Name_____

Magic Paint

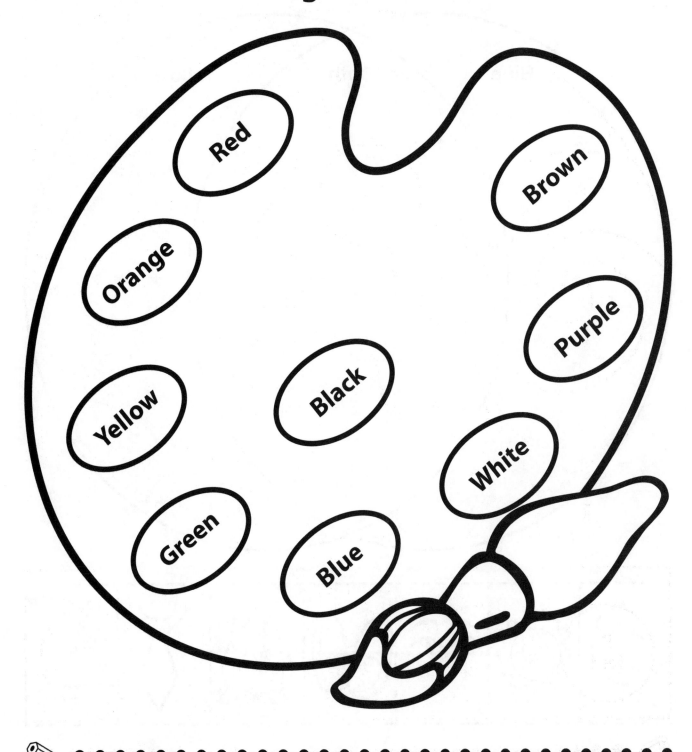

Directions: Read the color words. Color the paint palette and the brush.

Name_____

Color Sort

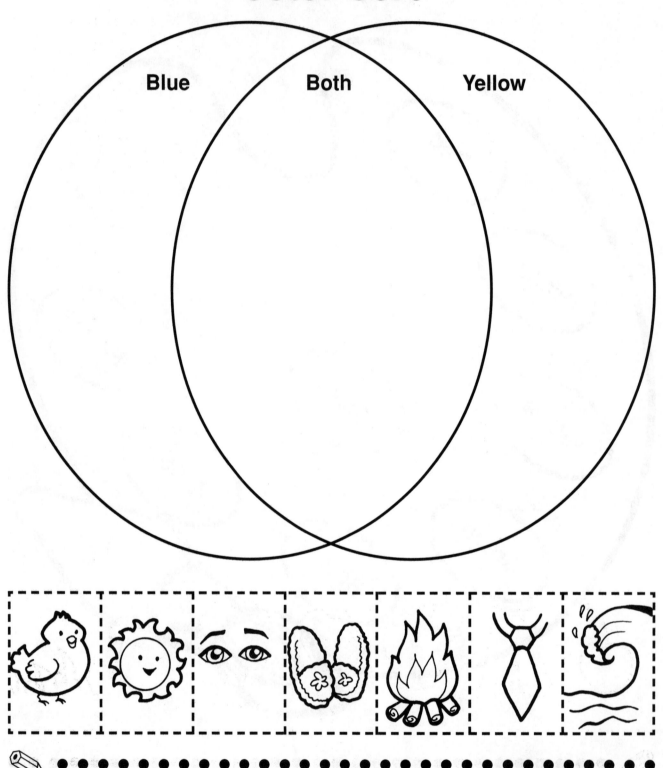

Blue   Both   Yellow

Directions: Cut out the boxes. Decide if the item should be blue or yellow, or if it can be either color. Glue the pictures into the color circle where they fit. Objects that can be either color should be placed in the middle, where both circles are joined.

Name_____

Color Sort 2

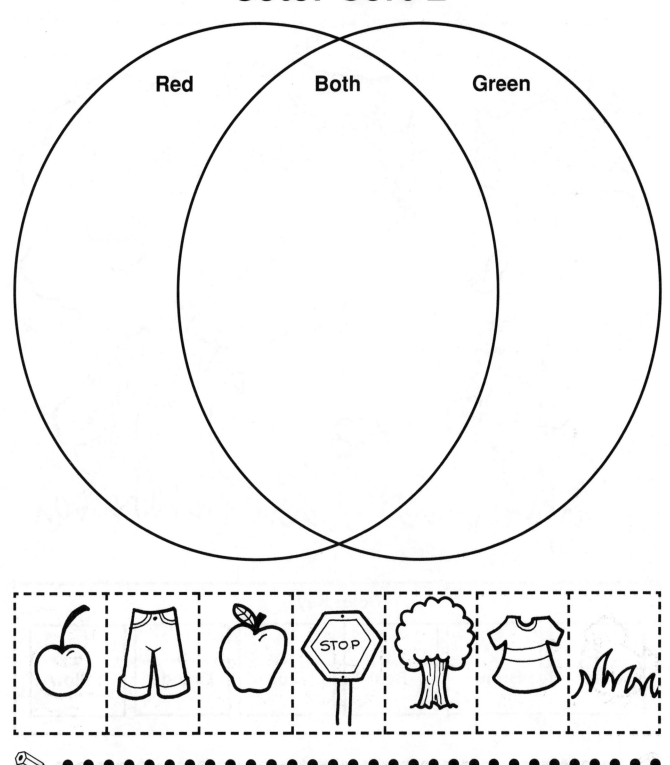

Red   Both   Green

Directions: Cut out the objects and decide what color each item should be. Glue the pictures in the correct place. Objects that can be either color should be placed in the middle where both circles are joined.

Name _____

Color Code

Color Key

1 Green	2 Brown	3 Red	4 Blue	5 Orange	6 Yellow

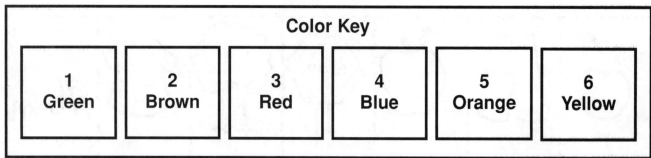

Directions: Color the Color Key. Color the picture using the Color Key.

Name_____

More Color Codes

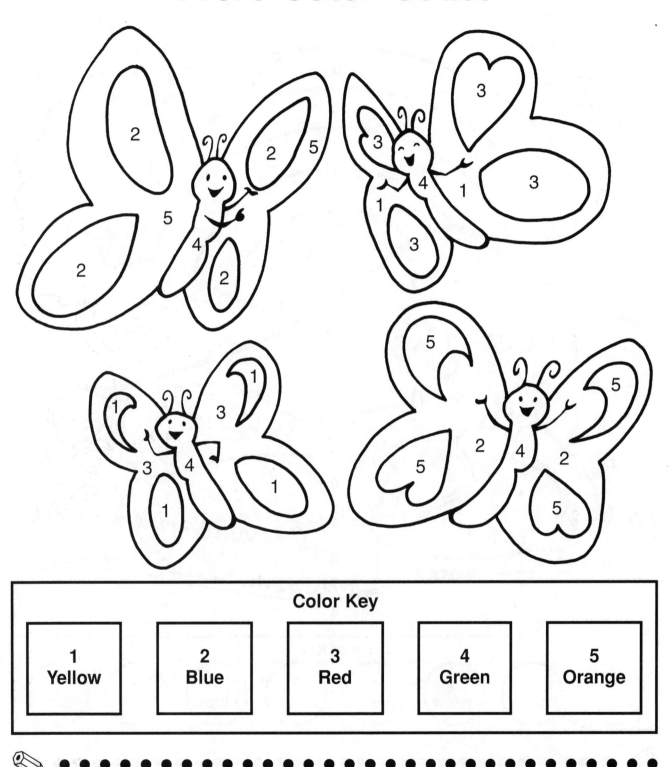

Color Key

| 1 Yellow | 2 Blue | 3 Red | 4 Green | 5 Orange |

Directions: Color the Color Key. Color the picture using the Color Key.

Color by Numbers

Color Key

1 Red	2 Orange	3 Yellow	4 Green	5 Blue	6 Purple	7 Brown	8 Gray

Directions: Color the Color Key. Each color has a number. Color the picture using the Color Key.

48